RECYCLING DAY

Edward Miller

Holiday House / New York

Between two buildings was
a vacant lot.
It was a nice, sunny place.

In the lot lived
a group of bugs.

A fly made his home
in a can.

A family of ants nested in a glass bottle.

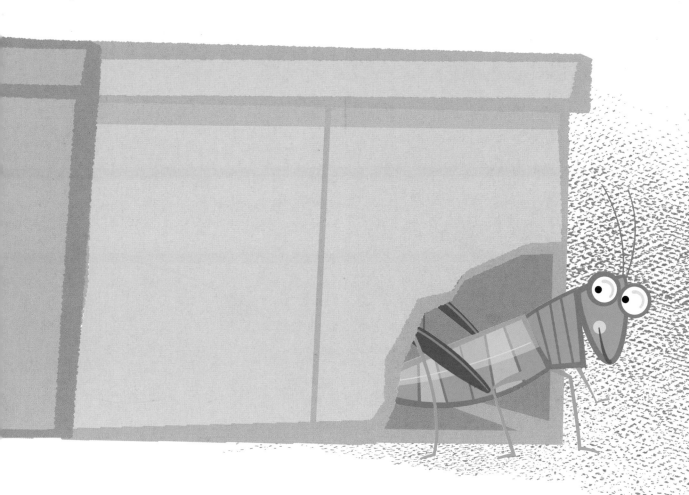

A grasshopper settled in a cardboard box.

And a worm dug in the
ground under some rocks.

People threw trash into the lot. At first it was small things.

But then bigger items were dumped such as shoes,
old computers, and bicycle tires. Before long the pile
of trash was higher than the fence.

Then the unthinkable happened. A gang of rats found the lot.

"This looks like the perfect disgusting place to live," said the boss rat. "Let's take over!"

The boss rat grabbed the worm by the throat and said, "From now on I'm in charge here!"

A hungry rat bullied the ants into giving him their lunches.

A lazy rat kicked the grasshopper out of his box.

And a nasty rat tried to swat the fly and eat him.

The bugs were terrified.

"We need to do something about these rotten rats," said the grasshopper.

"But how can we make them leave?" said the worm. "They love all this trash."

The bugs felt hopeless and defeated.

PROTECT YOUR HANDS— WEAR GARDENING GLOVES TO PICK UP TRASH!

Until one promising day wh
a girl posted a sign on the fence.
The sign read:

RECYCLING DAY

THIS SATURDAY
HELP US CLEAN
UP THIS LOT!

Volunteers did come. They brought containers, rakes, and work gloves.

The bugs were glad but not the rats. They scrambled out of sight.

The volunteers collected the bottles.
"Where are you taking our bottle?" asked the ants.
"This bottle is going to be recycled," the boy said.
"What does 'recycle' mean?" asked an ant.
"Recycle means to take something used, like this old bottle, melt it down with other bottles, then make new ones and reuse them," the boy explained.

"Recycling sounds like a good idea!" said the ants.

BE CAREFUL
NOT TO CUT
YOURSELF
ON BROKEN
GLASS!

GLASS RECYCLING

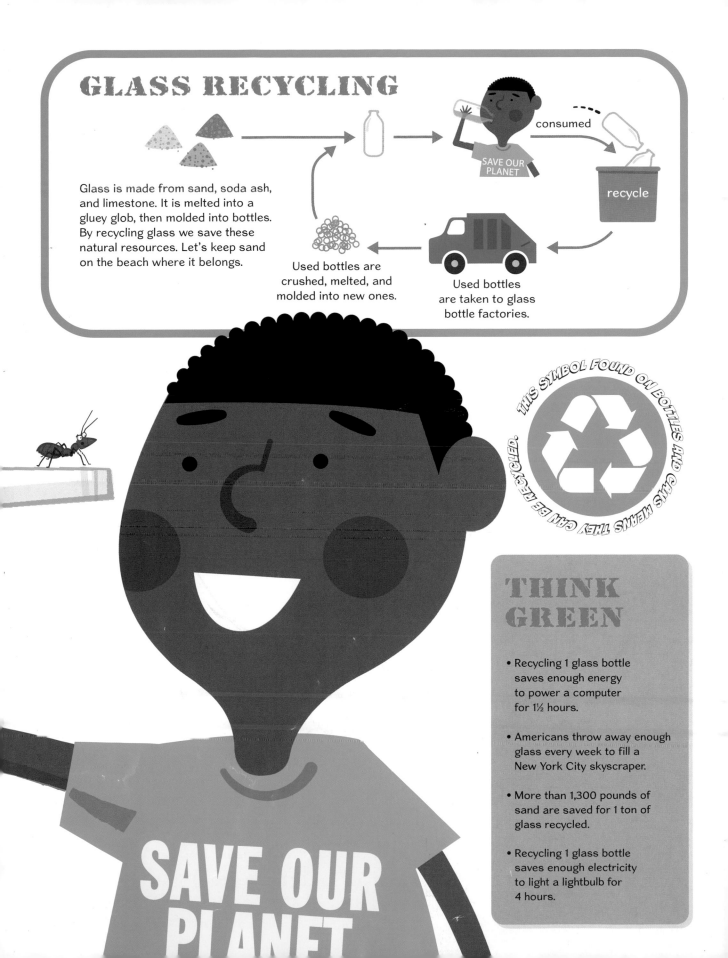

Glass is made from sand, soda ash, and limestone. It is melted into a gluey glob, then molded into bottles. By recycling glass we save these natural resources. Let's keep sand on the beach where it belongs.

consumed

recycle

Used bottles are crushed, melted, and molded into new ones.

Used bottles are taken to glass bottle factories.

SAVE OUR PLANET

THIS SYMBOL FOUND ON BOTTLES AND CANS MEANS THEY CAN BE RECYCLED.

THINK GREEN

- Recycling 1 glass bottle saves enough energy to power a computer for 1½ hours.

- Americans throw away enough glass every week to fill a New York City skyscraper.

- More than 1,300 pounds of sand are saved for 1 ton of glass recycled.

- Recycling 1 glass bottle saves enough electricity to light a lightbulb for 4 hours.

SAVE OUR PLANET

Volunteers gathered all the papers, newspapers, and cardboard boxes.

"What are you going to do with my box?" asked the grasshopper.

"This box will be recycled. It will be shredded and made into new cardboard. We save trees when we recycle paper and boxes," said the girl.

"Saving trees is a good idea!" said the grasshopper.

PAPER RECYCLING

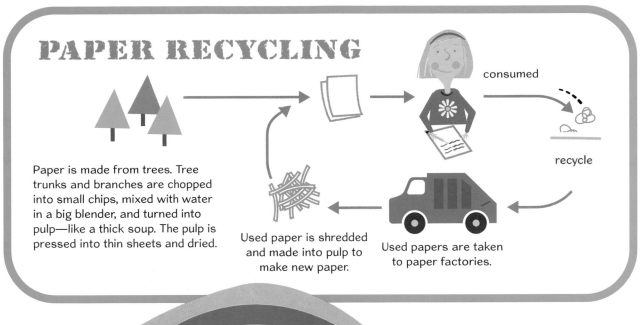

consumed

recycle

Paper is made from trees. Tree trunks and branches are chopped into small chips, mixed with water in a big blender, and turned into pulp—like a thick soup. The pulp is pressed into thin sheets and dried.

Used paper is shredded and made into pulp to make new paper.

Used papers are taken to paper factories.

THINK GREEN

- Nearly 4 billion trees are cut down each year to make paper.

- The average person uses enough paper in one year to need 7 trees to manufacture it.

- Americans discard 4 million tons of paper every year. That's enough to build a wall of paper 12 feet high from New York to California.

- Save wrapping paper to rewrap gifts.

- Reduce the amount of paper you use by writing on both sides.

- Each ton of recycled paper can save 17 million trees.

- Use old magazines to make crafts.

- Use dishes and cloth napkins instead of paper plates and napkins.

Volunteers also collected metal.

The fly put his can in the pile too. "What will happen to my can?" asked the fly.

"This can will be melted down with the others and molded into new ones," said the boy.

"I like shiny new cans," said the fly.

THINK GREEN

- More than 80 billion aluminum soda cans are used each year around the world.

- Americans use 100 million cans per day.

- Recycling 1 aluminum can saves enough energy to run a television for 3 hours.

- The energy saved each year by recycling cans could light Washington, DC for more than 3 years.

- More than 100,000 aluminum cans are recycled every minute of every day.

- An aluminum can thrown in a dump will still be there 500 years from now.

METAL RECYCLING

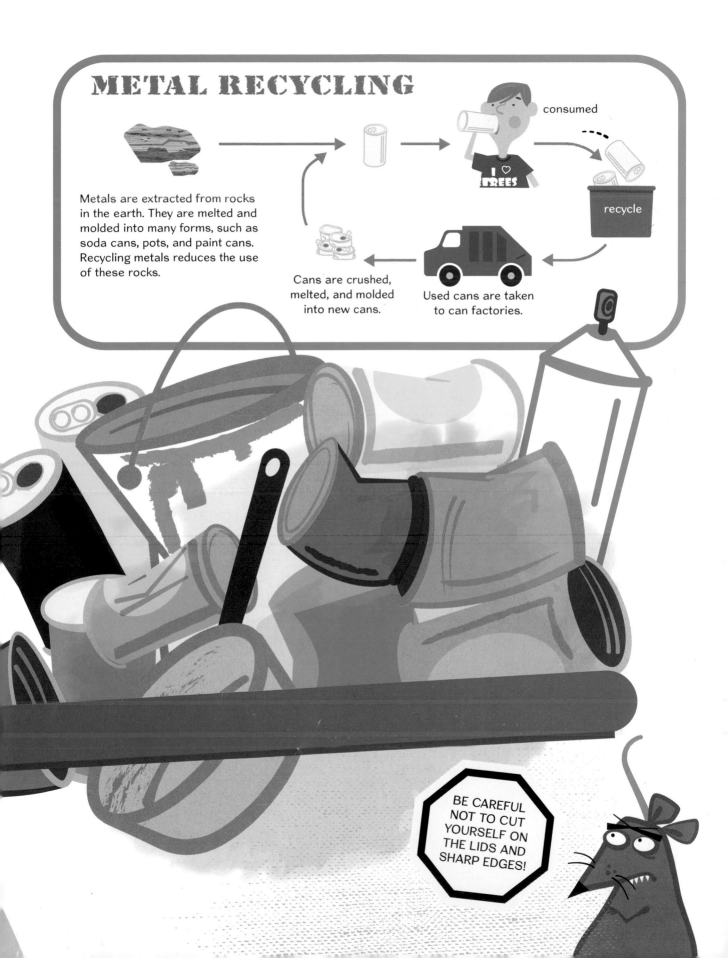

consumed

recycle

Metals are extracted from rocks in the earth. They are melted and molded into many forms, such as soda cans, pots, and paint cans. Recycling metals reduces the use of these rocks.

Cans are crushed, melted, and molded into new cans.

Used cans are taken to can factories.

BE CAREFUL NOT TO CUT YOURSELF ON THE LIDS AND SHARP EDGES!

The volunteers collected all the plastics they could find. "Plastics can be recycled too?" asked the bugs in surprise. "Yes!" replied a girl. "Plastic can be melted down and molded into all kinds of things, such as milk jugs, water bottles, and toys."

THINK GREEN

- Americans use 2½ million plastic bottles every hour! Most of them are thrown away!

- There is a mass of plastic pieces twice the size of Texas floating in the Pacific Ocean.

- Tons of plastic waste wash up on shores all over the world.

- Plastic can be dangerous to animals. Animals can mistake it for food, eat it, and choke.

- Enough plastic is made in the United States each year to shrink-wrap Texas.

- Enough plastic bottles are thrown away in the United States each year to circle the earth 4 times.

- Use reusable water bottles, shopping bags, and lunch bags.

- Reuse plastic containers to store your toys, crayons, and treasures.

PLASTIC RECYCLING

Plastics are made from mixing oil and a chemical called chlorine found in the earth's crust. Plastic is a strong, flexible material that doesn't break down over time.

consumed

recycle

Plastics are shredded, melted, and molded into new plastics.

Used plastics are taken back to plastic factories.

RINSE OUT PLASTIC CONTAINERS WITH WATER BEFORE YOU RECYCLE!

The volunteers put leaves and vegetable and fruit food scraps from their lunches into a compost bin.

"What is compost?" said the worm.

"Compost is a rich soil made with food scraps, leaves, and water. It is healthy food for plants and flowers," said the boy.

"Sounds like a nice place to make a home," said the worm.

THINK GREEN

• Vegetables and fruits grown in compost soil produce healthier foods for people to eat.

• Worms can help in the compost process. They eat the scraps, breaking it down into smaller pieces.

• Flowers, trees, and plants grow bigger and stronger in compost soil.

You Can Compost:
fruit cores
fruit and vegetable peels and scraps
corncobs
eggshells
pet fur
leaves
nut shells
pencil shavings
tea bags

Do Not Compost:
meat
bones
eggs
dairy products

The volunteers collected trash that could not be recycled for the garbage collector to take to the dump.

Do Not Recycle:
waxed paper
plastic wrap
candy wrappers
photo paper
dark-colored paper
broken glass
lightbulbs
sandwich bags
drinking straws
batteries
Styrofoam
mirrors

By the end of the day, the volunteers cleared the lot and planted a garden. They saved trees, sand, metals, and other natural materials by recycling. And they reduced the amount of trash headed for the dump.

The bugs loved the improvements, but the rats did not. They scrambled into a garbage pail to hide.

Then as luck would have it, the garbage collector picked up the trash. The rats tumbled into the back of the truck, and they were on their way to the dump.

The rats were never seen again, and the bugs enjoyed the garden.

THINK GREEN

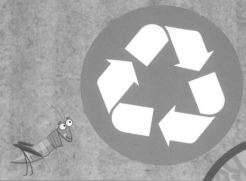

SAVE OUR PLANET

What else can we recycle?

Check with your local government for guidelines about how and what to recycle in your community.

TOYS
- Donate toys in good condition.
- Buy toys that come in packages that can be recycled. For example, choose a toy in a paperboard box instead of one packed in plastic.

ELECTRONICS AND BATTERIES
- Electronics and batteries are made from metals and plastics. They can poison the soil and water. It is important to keep electronics out of the dumps so this doesn't happen.
- Recycle or donate cell phones, video games, electronic toys, and cameras. Your town or city will likely have a recycling drive to collect these items.
- Don't buy the newest electronic device if the one you have is working fine.

FABRICS
- Recycle worn-out clothes, towels, sheets, shoes, and sneakers. Your town or city will likely have a recycling drive to collect these items.
- Donate clothes and shoes that are still good.
- Use old fabrics to make crafts. Old socks make good puppets and dolls.

BOOKS
- Donate used books to the library or share them with your friends.

GARBAGE BAGS CAN CAUSE SUFFOCATION! NEVER PUT ONE OVER YOUR FACE OR HEAD!

Note about Dumps

A dump (or landfill) is where our trash is taken. Dumps can be as big as football fields, but it does not take long to fill one to the top. Someday there will be no more room to dump all our trash.

    We can help reduce the amount of trash that goes to the dump by recycling. You will help make the earth a cleaner place to live.

Note about Littering

Careless people throw trash such as cans and candy wrappers on the ground. This is called littering. A person who litters is called a litterbug.

    Cans and bottles left on playgrounds and in parks can kill plants and harm children if stepped on.

    Some litter gets washed away when it rains and travels into rivers and oceans. Animals eat the garbage and get sick, and some die.

So, don't be a litterbug!
Together we can make the earth a safer place for plants, animals, and ourselves.

To my editor, Mary Cash, with
gratitude for guiding my career
—E. M.

HOLIDAY HOUSE is registered in the U.S. Patent and Trademark Office.
Printed and Bound in May 2014 at Tien Wah Press, Johor Bahru, Johor, Malaysia.
www.holidayhouse.com
First Edition
1 3 5 7 9 10 8 6 4 2

Library of Congress Cataloging-in-Publication Data
Miller, Edward, 1964– author, illustrator.
Recycling day / Edward Miller. — First edition.
pages cm
Summary: Bugs happily living in an empty lot are in trouble
when a gang of rats moves in and takes over, but when a group of volunteers
arrives to clean up, not only do the bugs get their lot back, they learn
about recycling, composting, and garbage dumps. Includes facts
about dumps, littering, and recycling.
ISBN 978-0-8234-2419-1 (hardcover)
[1. Recycling (Waste)—Fiction. 2. Sanitary landfills—Fiction.
3. Compost—Fiction. 4. Animals—Fiction.] I. Title.
PZ7.M61287Rec 2014
[E]—dc23
2014001893

Follow Ed Miller on Facebook at Ed Miller Design.